FIVE IRISH POETS

FIVE IRISH POETS

PADRAIG J. DALY
JOHN F. DEANE
RICHARD KELL
DENNIS O'DRISCOLL
MACDARA WOODS

Preface by Thomas Kinsella
Introduction by David Lampe
Edited by David Lampe and Dennis Maloney

White Pine Press
Dedalus Press

ISBN - 0-934834-99-7
Publication of this book was made possible, in part, by grants from
the National Endowment for the Arts and the New York State
Council on the Arts.

Design by Watershed Design
Cover Art by Robert Ballagh

White Pine Press
76 Center Street
Fredonia, NY 14063

Dedalus Press
24 The Heath
Cypress Downs
Dublin 6W Ireland

CONTENTS

RICHARD KELL

MACDARA WOODS

JOHN F. DEANE

PADRAIG J. DALY

DENNIS O'DRISCOLL

PREFACE

In the half century since Yeats' death there have been four 'generations' of Irish poets: one that was young and obscured during his late career; a later one that could feel the weight of his presence but with some hope, in the 1940s and after, of escape; and one that grew up in forced seclusion during the Second World War, not knowing much about an outside world, and knowing no more of Yeats than of any other major European writer of the pre-War years. Richard Kell is one of these. The other poets in this anthology come from a later generation still, born after Yeats' death, and for whom Yeats is only a great special figure out of the past.

But there is something in the direction of Yeats' career that affects all Irish poets writing in English. Producing, in some cases, poetry of the highest kind, they can find themselves addressing it away from the area of experience. It is the provincial predicament. For the country as a whole it is the post-Colonial predicament, with the work directed toward a primary audience elsewhere. Yeats, in an attitude accepted out of the Colonial past, directed his work from the beginning toward an outside audience. The related effects among subsequent writers have varied: from total isolation, as with Austin Clarke, to abnormal emphasis, as with Brendan Behan, delighting in the role of native performer; most recently, in a provincial Ulster poetic Renaissance addressing its work toward the British mainland and finding an identity there.

There has been a related experience in publishing. Until the 1950s Irish poets were at the mercy of publishing circumstance, their work taken up, or not, by British publishing houses according as the Irish aspect was found acceptable or interesting. The natural dynamics of a writer's development in some kind of contact with an audience sharing some kind of understanding were interfered with.

In the 1950s the Dolmen Press in Dublin approached this matter directly. During Yeats' anniversary, we are remembering another death, that of Liam Miller, founder of the Dolmen Press and a creative figure in Irish publishing, the first to provide professional publication in Ireland for a modern Irish poetry and giving Austin Clarke, in the process, an honorable and lively end to his career. But there was a problem of scale. The purchasing audience in Ireland is a small one, too small to justify the full-scale publication of major books. This problem was solved by a partnership arrangement with other publishers distributing outside of Ireland. The essential limitations remained, however, and showed

1

themselves again after Miller's death. The Dolmen Press was the product of individual energy and genius, and it disappeared with him.

It is here that the Dedalus Press is valuable, with the professional publication of new books by Irish poets; and also with this anthology. In the cooperation between Dedalus and the White Pine Press the problem of scale is being faced again.

Five Irish Poets offers a selection of some of the new poetry of Ireland. It is difficult to generalize about the selection as a whole. One can only welcome it and look forward to other books of the same kind. But perhaps one thing might be said about all five writers. The world they present is one of settled attitudes, and they share a tendency toward settled methods; but it is an uneasy world. Richard Kell, born in 1927, grew up during the isolation of the war years. Dennis O'Driscoll, youngest poet in the selection, was born in 1954 and grew up during the development of a new Europe, where a war like the Second World War would seem unthinkable. The selection might be read as a documentary: of seclusion; of reaction to the excesses of the Century; of hesitation now in the face of everything, including a Europe that is integrating in non-violent but threatening ways. Ireland is a small country at the edge of the continent, but these poems show that it has not been spared any of the experience of the time.

--Thomas Kinsella

INTRODUCTION

There is no mantle
and it does not descend
    --Thomas Kinsella

As Robert Graves and Laura Riding once put it, "The Anthology of the days before cheap books were printed was justified as a secure portfolio for short poems that might otherwise be lost." And certainly the *Greek Anthology* and *Carmina Burana* have provided us with unique and vital poems that might otherwise have been lost. Yet after the age of cheap books another tradition emerged, that of Palgrave's *Golden Treasury* (1861) or of Quiller-Couch's *Oxford Book of English Verse* (1900). These anthologies presumed to establish "all the best original Lyrical pieces and Songs in our language...and none beside the best" as Palgrave, following the metrics of Tennyson, immodestly puts it. To achieve this public canonization of private taste, editors were often willing to mangle the text of poems. "I have often excised weak superfluous stanzas when sure that excision would improve," Quiller-Couch coyly admits. And violence does not end there, for anthologies can be examples of imperialistic aggrandizement or even undeclared acts of war. One need only recall the rear guard action of Yeats' *Oxford Book of Modern Verse* (1939) or the recent inclusion of Seamus Heaney in a book of "British poetry" to see how politically charged the act of editing can be.

In 1962, in quite a different manner, the English/Canadian scholar and poet Robin Skelton brought out an important selection, *Six Irish Poets*, which included Thomas Kinsella, John Montague, Richard Murphy, Austin Clarke, Richard Weber and Richard Kell. This was an important and valiant effort of editorship and enterprise which gave attention to both recognized and emerging talent. Indeed, it may be that at that moment of Irish literary history, only an outsider would have had the privilege of honest enthusiasm without danger of partisan prejudice.

Recently the appearances of anthologies by Paul Muldoon (1986) and Thomas Kinsella (1987) have underlined the potential political, polemical and poetical hazards that confront an editor. Reviewers criticized Muldoon for being too selective and Kinsella for being too idiosyncratically insistent on a thesis in his selections and translations. Yet in both of these cases the anthologies have special fascination for they allow us to observe major poets make

3

their selection and consequently acknowledge their own literary histories be it North or South; Belfast or Dublin; Gaelic, Latin, or English; private or public.

Yet poets do not merely create their literary worlds in anthologies and not all anthologists are poets or Palgraves. The recent history of Irish publishing, reviewed above by Thomas Kinsella, suggests another important avenue for expression and nurturing. The aim of this anthology of Irish poets is to introduce a group of poets published by Dedalus Press who, though still widely various in their experiences and expressions share a number of concerns. It provides a sympathetic, though not uncritical, selection of post-Modern Irish poetry and introduces to both Irish and American audiences a group of poets whose works deserve attention and will repay reading.

The senior poet of this collection, Richard Kell, was born in Youghal in 1927, educated in Belfast and Trinity College, Dublin. He taught at Isleworth Polytechnic from 1960-69 and from 1970 till 1983 was senior lecturer at Newcastle-upon-Tyne Polytechnic. His books include an early appearance in *Fantasy Poets 35* (Oxford, 1957), followed by *Control Tower* (1962), *Differences* (1969), *Humours* (1978), *Heartwood* (1978), and *Praise of Warmth* (1987).

His mastery of form still allows for expression of intense personal emotion which ranges from mourning to sensual surprise; or as he puts it in "At Glen Coe: 1976," he hears and records

no 'still, sad music,' but the piercing skirl
of nerve and passion fined to artfulness.
I hear the folk tunes drifting down the glen
and can't forget the treacherous courtesy
that ended in a massacre.

Macdara Woods was born in Dublin in 1942 and began publishing poetry while an undergraduate at University College, Dublin. In 1975 he co-founded *Cyphers,* which he still co-edits. As befits a modern troubadour he has had a range of jobs and travelled to many exotic places. Passionately intense yet playful, his poetry is filled with a range of experiences and localities and makes reference to works as diverse as Ariosto and Bob Dylan. His poems mix the cryptically ironic with the domestic and chic as they call forth jovial nightmares:

I called to my wife starting out for work
could you take my head in to town today please

have my hair cut and my beard trimmed
for this poetry reading on Thursday
(I was dusting my high-heeled Spanish boots)

John F. Deane was born on Achill Island in 1943 and educated at
University College, Dublin. He taught secondary school in Dublin
until 1979 when he organized *Poetry Ireland*. In 1985 he founded
Dedalus Press. He has been especially active in translating and
publishing European poets: Sweden's Tomas Transtromer, Ruma-
nia's Marin Sorescu, Denmark's Uffe Harder, and Yugoslavia's Ivan
Lalic. His own books include *Stalking After Time* (1977); *High
Sacrifice* (1981); *Winter in Meath* (1985); *Road, With Cypress and
Star* (1988). A late starter as a poet, he brings to the literary life
intense and focused energy. "The sense of poetry as a life's task, as
a commitment that is passionate, probing and integrate, is too
rare," he has said, but Deane's own commitment to his life's task, to
his own poetry, to his translating, and to his publishing firm and
Poetry Ireland have, as this collection makes clear, made an
important difference. As Thomas Kinsella suggests, his Dedalus
Press is the successor to Liam Miller's Dolmen Press.

Padraig J. Daly, born in Dungarvan, County Waterford in 1943,
is an Augustinian priest working in Dublin. He has published
Nowhere But in Praise (1978) and *This Day's Importance* (1981).
His *Selected Poems* appeared from Dedalus Press in 1988. His
works have been translated into Italian by Marguerita Guidacci
and published in Rome. His poems range from imagistic evocations
of an Irish autumn

How trees suddenly turn gold
And drop their beauty
Spendthrift to earth

to meditations on Francis and Augustine;

And nowhere but in praise
Can quark or atom
Or any fraction else of mass
Find peace.

The youngest poet of this collection is Dennis O' Driscoll, who
was born in Thurles, County Tipperary in 1954. He has published
concise and valuable criticism in *Agenda, Crane Bag,* and *Sunday
Tribune.* I first heard of him from a Dublin bookstore owner who

hailed him as an honest, independent reviewer with probing intelligence and poetic sensitivity. These qualities are also apparent in his two collections of poems, *Kist* (1982) and *Hidden Extras* (1987) where

> revelation strikes occasionally:
> a glimmer of wisdom shimmering. . .
> an inkling of transcendence in a momentary hush.

Though these five poets may not wear the elusive mantle of endorsed poetic succession, their descent is Irish and they speak with voices that deserve to be heard.

--David Lampe
August 1989

RICHARD KELL

THE SWAN

Nothing more serene than the fluid neck,
the body curved like snow on foliage,
and spilt reflection moving smooth as oil.

But something wrecks the tranquil certainty:
the clean-cut shape unfolds; an evil wind
tears its roots out of the fertile water.

The pattern's tugged awry - the neck rammed stiff,
cumbrous wings whacking the startled air -
and terror swirls the surface of the lake.

ENCOUNTER IN A READING ROOM

Good luck has entered, silky and black, padding
slowly towards the desk where I sit reading.
And idly superstitious I think 'Supposing
she came to me, sensing that I'm uneasy,
singled me out for comfort and change of fortune',
yet know her poised contempt is all but certain.

Yes, like a brief sensation she goes by
and out of sight: why should she favour me
among so many strangers with sorrows, fears
like mine? I try to read - though feeling blurs
the glass of understanding time and again,
for all the will's concern to wipe it clean -

but look, she turns and springs, the logic gives
beneath her sudden weight! And now she curves
and ripples in my arm, her grappling claws
tear at my sleeve; the green uncanny eyes,
slotted with black, distil an arctic glare,
and endlessly her soft vibrating purr

winds intimacy off a reel of distance.
So she has come, indulging my pretence
of singularity and special need.
And let her now pretend my gratitude
in one final amused caress, before
I drop self-pity gently on the floor.

THE TOWER AND THE OCEAN

To feel the wind up there
purling on those great battlements, I entered
the numb and stony darkness, and began to
trudge the coiled stair.

Heard, half way up, the sound
of scrubbing-brush and pail, where Mrs. Crone
worked her poor fingers to the bone
in her long daily round.

The steps were hard and cold
on which she knelt, plying her only skill
year after year, and talking gaily still
though tired and old.

No stir of life but hers. On the top floor,
roneo, box-file, desk and balance sheet
furnished a room impersonal and neat
beyond an open door.

I turned to climb - above me the sweet air,
the final twist of stone. The way was barred,
and in black letters on a card
Not Open to the Public printed there.

A loophole shone in darkness: down below,
the tennis balls were soaring, floating, and
the players reaching up in a big wind -
their rippling tunics dazzled me like snow -

and mounds of sapphire, flaring into white,
drowned half the sky in waves
whose crumbling scarps and luminous glissades
filled all my veins with light.

GOSPEL TOWN

Under its hump the town
endures nightfall. Sand
sweats as the tide uncovers
drainage and slimy stone.
Fairylights, fountain, bandstand
play the uneasy lovers.

Their ingrown hungers rage:
hot sermons, anodyne
of hymns, disturb the patter
of the hypnotist on the stage,
where tranced lips guzzle wine
from glasses filled with water.

Pure streams from granite ledges
fall through the glens, and swill
flat shingle solitudes
beyond the last bridges.
Unfathomably still
the black mountain broods.

SKY POEM

Taking off, he's glad of the rough power
  he has little use for: the towing plane
bullies both wind and spirit, but like a ripsaw
  slices along their grain.

At two thousand feet he drops the cable,
  feels the glider float free -
air sliding and whispering over wings
  like an ideal sea.

He plays off gravity against the surge of wind,
  moves the controls lightly to steer
uncalculated courses, true to the subtle
  weave of the atmosphere.

And knows the signs, the promises: where he sees
  a puff of cumulus he can soar
in slow circles on the rising heat.
  But nothing delights him more

than the unexpected gift of a blue thermal
  suddenly taking hold of the plane
in its long glide down, like a soft explosion
  urging it up again.

Sometimes, though, the sky turns sulky,
  withdraws her lithe and buoyant air:
the flier, for all his art, can only droop
  to a field in the middle of nowhere.

WALKING WITH MATRON

In the Nilgiris, a platoon of Christ's cadets
with uniform shirts and topee helmets, we were
marched under tropical leaves by Matron, singing
'Stand up, stand up for Jesus'. She led us firmly
out of the hooting shadows to revelations
of sky and mountain, precipices with slow white
ropes of water dropping three thousand feet to the
empty plain, and we rested there in the silence
that calmed her voice as she told us about the one
sheep that was lost and found. We filled our
                              handkerchiefs
with tea berries, put beetles like gems in boxes
velveted with moss. On the way back I managed
not to crunch my peppermint: it dissolved on my
tongue like a sliver of ice, and my bitten mouth
was cool and peaceful. But near the school we halted,
while Matron lifted her walking-stick and battered
a small brown snake to death, her spectacles glowing.

SABBATH TRIPTYCH

Music by Wagner: horns and violins
propose the condonation of his sins
who honoured God the Logos. Mr. Smith
would rather have a car to tinker with,
a hedge to trim, and God the Mechanist -
aloof, the cosmos ticking on his wrist.
Between the radio and electric shears,
myself and two Jehovah's Witnesses
contending on the doorstep. 'It's all here
in black and white, the prophecies are clear'
they tell me, shaking dust off, snapping God
the Father in a briefcase. Overhead
the unclouded sunlight equably surveys
its colours redisposed a thousand ways.

TRY YOUR STRENGTH

Alone, supine, each of us left in peace
with the lid down. Heaven and hell
in a nauseous equilibrium, unbearable.
So the will moves, the blood prepares for action.

No justice weighed these plates of rock.
Some people flip them open,
switching the sunlight on;
others have to heave with their whole strength
to gain a slow illumination;
a few press and press on the dead stone
until their souls ache -
purchase at best a brief flicker,
slump back into themselves, and stare
for hours in the numb dark,
longing to fall asleep and never wake.

LOFTHOUSE COLLIERY, 1973

Somebody yelled *Get out!* as the coal-face split,
and thousands of lethal tons began to pour
from the black fathoms of an abandoned pit.
The miners raced from its terrible breath and roar
through half a mile of darkness. Young Cotton ran
beyond danger, but in agony of mind,
praying with every stride that his old man,
'a bit buggered in the wind', plodding behind,
would live, yet knew there wasn't a hope in hell -
and what could *he* do by turning back, but make
two deaths instead of one... His father fell
as the packed water slammed him: *For God's sake
run, boy, run!* was his last cry
before his lips were muffled; then he gave
his lonely mind to whatever it meant to die
buried already in a violent grave.

SPRING NIGHT
(for M.)

Out on Killiney Hill that night, you said
'Remember how we promised to come up here
when snow is lying under a full moon?'
And I made no reply - to hide my sadness,
thinking we might not satisfy that whim,
ever perhaps, at least for years to come,
since it was spring, and winter would see us parted.

Sitting on the Druid's Chair recalled
the last time we were there, a night of icy
wind and moonlight when the sea was churning
silver and the distant hills were clear;
how we belonged to them and they to us.
Now there was no brightness - only a vast
obscurity confusing sea and sky,
Dalkey Island and the lights of Bray
submerged and suffocating in the mist.

And there was no belonging now; no vivid
elemental statement to compel
refusal or assent, making decision
easy; but a dumb neutrality
that challenged us to give it character
and view our own minds large as a landscape.
To you it was tranquil. Sinister to me.

Lying under the pine tree, looking up
at the small stars and breathing the wood's sweetness,
we spoke hardly a word. I could not tell you
I was afraid of something out there
in the future, like that dark and bitter sea;
and how my love for you would have me lonely
until the fear was broken. I could say
'Be close to me next winter and every winter;

we'll come up here to watch the snow by moonlight' -
and that would be too easy. For I must give
to you whose meaning transcends moods and

moments

nothing half-hearted or ambiguous,
but the perfected diamond of my will.

(1952)

THE RESCUE

(in memorium M.K.)

Gentle, warm, dark, the sea
you rocked her in; dreadful
the fire your love became
to give her breath. But once
wasn't enough, it seems:
what providence conceives
a crux like this? - the child
delivered into pain,
you strangling in warped floods,
the labour of your birth
into final stillness.

MARRIAGE IS LIKE A TREE
(in memorium M.K.)

After the flood, its roots are dying in air.
When twenty-two rings of tough growth
fell in a race of water,
the bark was lumpy with healed wounds,
the heartwood sound.

I recall, with a love that's inward now,
its many changes: foliage playing
in light, drooping in damp glooms
or stilled by rich calms of summer;
branches furred with snow, or their stormy thrashing.

How sad, these emptied places. But elsewhere
you find, again with sadness, trees that were hurt
too deeply, unnerved by pest and fungus,
hollowing to their last stand
against the rising wind.

It could be a kind of luck, being left
the ghost of a scarred tree
still healthy when it toppled:
leaves whispering through all the mind's seasons,
a root safe in the ground for ever.

AT GLEN COE: 1976

A place for tourists now. In the parking bay
tires crunch to a standstill. Cameras wink
at a piper massive as a monument,
cutting him down to size for snapshot albums.
But on the bridge below, by a dark pool
and a rowan tree, you hear the edgy sweetness
of chant and drone mix with the tangled notes
of water spilling endlessly on rock.
The rich primordial bourdon of the mind
begins its dreamy monotone: absorbed
in ancient stillnesses, you'd think the cries
and pistol shots echoed from icy crags
less than three hundred years ago meant nothing.
But mind grew into self, became aware
of selves, of kind and unkind, consonance
and dissonance - above the steady hum
no 'still, sad music', but the piercing skirl
of nerve and passion fined to artfulness.
I hear the folk tunes drifting down the glen
and can't forget the treacherous courtesy
that ended in a massacre. Kindest friend,
you know me now - hopeful when we're together,
loving the fells, the rivers, helping you
across the brimming stones; but every day
this radiant summer I've remembered death
and ways of dying - how natural kinship too
is torn by violence. While you gather cotton
from dried quagmire, I think of one whose children
swam with her in the sea she felt a part of
and saw the ungentle water stop her breath.

DEATH'S REPLY

I am not proud, nor do I seek dominion;
I do not destroy, or even sting.
Fire stings, and the nettle, and the scorpion;
violence breeds in every natural thing.

Innocent killers, you thrive on flesh or fruit;
guilty, you wreck and murder. You, not I,
sprang from the same imperishable root
as the wild energies of earth and sky.

Of the soul's destiny I know nothing;
but it may be, some part of you will thirst
for my Lethean purity, my soothing
emptiness, when life has done its worst.

TWO TREES
(for L.M.)

Widower now, uneasy in the stern,
trying to learn contentment as you row
across the liquid light,
I keep in memory how she took her turn
at the oars on the same lake -
and then how you and I
stood this morning on the shore,
amazed by naked roots
not intertwining merely, but grown together
into one organism,
yet oak and sycamore perfectly themselves.
These things were signs and mysteries once.
I think 'Two partners', then 'Two partnerships' -
and hold that sweet suggestion in my mind,
trying to hope, trying to learn belief
in a time without conviction.
You take your turn, the oars cutting deeply.
Light on the lifting blades breaks and falls.

THE BUTTERFLY HEARS TCHAIKOVSKY

Did it blunder in from the street?
Worse, imagine it reborn
among the platform flowers,
the first venture of delicate wings
wafting it straight to hell.
Our minds flooded with metaphor -
Francesca, Paolo, the manic winds
they're whirled in, all music
out of a soul in torment -
we watch that silky flier
lost in the glare, bewildered by
the shock of storming brass.
Flickering, it soars, dips,
traverses, its frail career
scribbled on art in a real
violence. When the applause breaks
it's gone - twitching perhaps
beside a player's foot, finished off
by the tuba's final blast,
the sumptuous crash of gong and cymbals.

Women! Persons! *Please!* Allow me to speak
just for a moment... Thank you... What I wanted
to say was this. To begin with, I understand.
No, I mean it: I do understand, and even
sympathize. In fact I'd go so far
as to call myself, with your permission of course,
a feminist. But there are, if I may say so,
feminists and feminists. Most of you here,
judging by what I've heard, would like to treat
men as they've treated women. I'm not surprised.
Age after grisly age of patriarchal
pride, insensitivity, exploitation -
no wonder you are militant! But consider:
has anything of enduring value ever
been gained by retaliation? Think, my friends!
Why would you take for model the sex you scorn?
Doing as they did, how would you help the world?
Cry out in protest, not in revenge and malice.
Firmly resist, but only in the name
of co-operation, sharing, mutual care,
equality, gentleness, all the lovely ways
that you can teach us now. We want to learn,
believe me. We *need* to learn if the human race
is not to... Thank you, ladies. Thanks for listening.
You're very kind... Thank you. I wish you well.

THE LIFE OF BRIAN

Brian, employed in Saudi Arabia, favours
rigorous laws and the chopping off of hands,
but finds it a rewarding sideline
to sell illegal liquor.
Recounting which, I add with smug humility,
lifting a packet of Marlboro, 'Of course
I can't throw stones: relying on these
is just as bad in a way.'
'Worse,' a friend obliges, and explains
with quiet authority that the land
cultivated by the tobacco barons
could have been used to feed the poor.
Right. And though he doesn't say so,
who but a hypocrite
would nod to his opinions while diffusing
a shifty veil of smoke?
Brian, frankly contemptuous of caring
for any but number one -
doing quite nicely money-wise,
enjoying far from his wife
a supply of emancipated nurses,
and keen, for his future security,
on the restoration of hanging
in the United Kingdom - puts me to shame.
Personal enterprise is more appealing
than indolent goodwill.
I'll shove my store of twenties
firmly into the dustbin, doing my bit
for the Third World, and rising
a notch or two in my friend's judgment.
Yes. Quite soon. When I'm feeling up to it.

THE BAY

Tuning that vague shrillness
above the sea's hiss,
you make out cells of melody
like the raw, tentative
music of genesis.

Then you reach sand, look up,
see the whole cliff
tingling with birds, and hear
their jubilant clarinets
playing a single riff:

the only notes they've made
from resonance that stirred
in bluegreens and in sea-lulled
leathery fronds before
the first cry was heard;

that keeps in just relation
different kinds, and brings
old and new together -
cradling flesh in rock,
filling the air with wings;

and now coaxes out
from room and car, to breathe
the tang of origins
where fish rot on shingle
and poisonous waters seethe,

Sapiens - who moved
fast into his own
wayward history, generating
seeds of fire and language,
fashioning blades of stone.

Here he puts his eye
to sandstone chinks, gazes
into uncanny chambers -
opium visions,
Piranesian mazes -

like the intricacies
of self and memory
by which he became aware
of death, invented heaven,
learned to plan and worry.

Programmed for work and play,
determined to feel free,
he browns oiled urban muscles
under the sky's grill,
and rides the tainted sea.

Caved in the cliffside pub
he stares across the bay,
and hears canned music, over
the wild calls, lamenting
'What made you go that way?'

Cradling glass in flesh,
he feels his mind slide
back towards timeless codes
that taught eyes to observe
and wings to glide;

but is boxed in his car again
as the daylight dulls -
quick-changer and polluter,
leaving far behind
the algae, the herring gulls.

TO LAUREN NEWLY BORN
(also for Jan and Eddie)

Lauren, your name is lovely -
that *l* and *r* and *n*
a chime melting on water,
easing the hearts of men.

It comes from distant ages
when leaves were heavenly signs,
and Petrarch made it timeless
in passion-haunted lines.

After the sleepy days,
the suckling and the weaning,
you'll give it year by year
your own rich meaning.

I send you now, for love,
a song as small as you,
wishing you faith and courage
whatever life may do.

COMING OF AGE
(for J.H.)

Though I have seldom slept alone, sharing
has never been quite like this.
Even now I jib at words
like ecstasy, rapture, bliss -
but let them go, let all we make together
speak for itself. I had this gift
from the others too - the dark delight when power
crests and spills - but left their own need drifting.
Selfish where they were humble,
I lingered only with my hands and eyes,
careless of what, assured as Venus, you
exult in. Drawing now your silvery cries,
I could teach myself-when-young a thing or two.

MACDARA WOODS

CAUCHEMAR IS A WHITE HORSE

Wear your hair like a skull cap
burning your brain; lay shoulders bare
like horses to hunger and thirst upon my energy,
for death and disease the offered groin.
One thousand years of horses' hooves
are beating here between twin stars
my eyes: come Cauchemar and ride our nights,
sweat yellow, sweet in the light lifting
from the eyes of Christ crossed in wire
staring in an ivy wind. Come Christ and Cauchemar,
my sweet mares till morning.

THE DRUNKEN LADIES

There was one drunken lady in Dublin
who ginned to sleep and cried
tell me love if we wake in the morning
but the boat had gone, the passage paid,
somebody slipped on the Dublin line.
There were five drunken ladies in Bayswater
the first was a red man's red-haired daughter
or maybe his wife it was no great matter
when four were drunk then one was sober,
there were three drunken ladies in Fulham
who had gone when he went back to London again,
there were two drunken ladies in Paris but
no time to stop to ask their names
for the train was leaving the station and
there was one drunken lady in Spain.

THE SIXTEENTH KIND OF FEAR

Who was it moving the curtain then?
Only the wind; the hand of the wind.

And who was it making light dance in the wind?
Only the sea-light caressing the sun.

Who was that walking when night came down?
Just a night-watchman thinking of home.

And whose was the face at my mountain window?
Only a dead tree white as a bone.

Whose was the fever then, cold in the sun?
Only my love's when my love lies alone.

And who is the stranger I meet in the evening?
Only the future, love, coming and going.

CONTROLLED AND INTERMITTENT FALLING

I'm sailing my hoist 15 stories up
watching the truth through a chink in the boards
a piece of dislodged concrete turning slowly
like a lazy killer fish in water sinking down
the levels of floors
and if you were to ask I'd say
my circles of experience spiral in
like a zoomshot on a staircase -
dizzy to look up and dangerous to look down.
What wind will form me patterns now,
eccentric circles, fragments of stone?
perhaps the dancers and the strangers
who refuse to get it straight
the legend on my doorway reads
London: Cul de Sac.
turning the wheel by opposites they sharpened steel
for a punctured lung on a railway bridge,
an eye gouged out and sepsis from a dirty knife;
the houses shrinking on a razor's acid edge,
arterial roads, two rooms, a telly set;
Thursday noon, pay packets and perhaps a bet,
Guinness and Bitter - the leering Black and Tan -
offense, surprise if you object;
thing is that we were doing our best
to keep a troubled ship together
on bad sea roads where each port seemed
less likely than another.
A tree in Green Park must make do for a forest
a pool set in mortar make do for an ocean
a street full of windows must make do for sand dunes,
the one action open is captive; is walking
without speaking, without stopping, without turning.
and so, from fifteen stories up
some lives become apparent. A definition:
controlled and intermittent falling.

DERRYRIBEEN. WESTPORT, JUNE 16th 1975

I pray you peace, you household gods
while daylight lasts; and the globed lamp burns.
today with trowelled hands I picked
mortar from between the bricks;
dust of years on your packed earth floor;
congealed; new smoke from the sunken grate
stormed like Djinns through the wall,
fingered a lapsed corner of the thatch;
your gallery three oleographs, a pope, two saints,
and good enough for Greco's ecstasies.
this cruel-toothed trowel proceeds
along the surfaces, the crevets, the edge of stone
interstices; I come upon a hollow place -
a rooted, peasant, catacomb,
and here, I see, you hid your folded hair,
the seasoned clippings of your nails,
pathetic, nameless, but remembered etcets.
all marked collect.
I offer you no hurt & nor do I disturb, distract.
this evening, quiet as sleeping trees,
household gods; I pray your peace.

VADE MECUM

Sailing half-over the indigo sea
think of me winging past the Crofton Hotel & the
                                                Comet
and remember you're to bring me back
snake-skin jackets, barn owls and alligators,
hoots of trains for my funeral
- sometime in the future -
&, Particularly, the brake-man, you know him
quote flagging down the Double E's
and come back to Erin - to empties, the cat,
full refuse sacks and me...
not everyone would see you go so quietly
-dial a mug on the subway -
they joked, I see no joking in it,
time-less, in the middle of the night
I sit with an empty glass, the 'phone,
and make to write a poem:
St. Paul in Minnesota on my birthday -
have an ironic drink for Baudelaire and me,
Scott Fitzgerald's gin and tonic
or Martini or Bourbon oh how Martinis nearly killed
                                                me,
or knowing me a pint of beer,
cerveza - the largest you can find:
take good care of yourself, beware the hospitality
and I'll do like for like in kind

CASSANDRA SPEAKS ABOUT THE IRISH FAMINE

Give me that sharp knife, the butcher's cutlass
that shall lacerate your womb,
do not endear me when the knives are sharp
do not sleep easy in your homes;
by times the night-winds slip in easy
and occupy your beds
the dead horse and the dead rider
are threatening your gods. What distaff
would you offer in the compound! Tchah!
would it even matter - a whiff in the nostril -
I speak of blood and a universe that couldn't listen,
there is blue-stone in the mountains -
in spring rivers gold glitters
think before you make a time of rags and flitters
& hand me that sharp knife, the butcher's cutlass,
better to cut out the sore
than die, begotten, eating reeds in ditches.

O BAKELITE MIZ MOON

Jump a hundred times
and then get laid
this is no horror movie
but late at night and I'm afraid
I tried to say I couldn't sleep
a bottle to my mouth
but looking backward over time
there's no sense of drought
& I believed you when you told me
that all green cheques were green -
green-backs, slap a dollar
this lady has been seen
in Banks with her machine-gun
holding up her own
I will salute you and respect you
oh bakelite Miz Moon.
A heart-break on the telephone
sparks off a certain lapse
a gentle lady in her cradle
an age, a meaning, and a breast;
we must have met light-years back
by the evil-winded sea
when you displayed your cuff-links
in your bed of porphyry,
did you amid the daylight
when the hours had crawled away
& they locked you in the close wing -
- every Swan must have her day -
find it written on the ceiling
as a moustache curling outward
a black and nonsense notion
did you find my lips too turgid
in the sex-scenes in the Motel
where we played Bianca Jaggers
sate Doctors of Divinities
and nurses at your elbow

while we reckoned hours in ounces
and made it down the highway
& I believed you when you told me
that the road had no horizon
as you smiled beneath your vizor
as you checked your magazine
and you got us to tomorrow
my sweet bakelite Miz Moon.

EIGHT HOURS TO PROVE THE ARTEFACT

Well now Miz Moon
do you remember what you recollected
& you remaining (still American) intact?
let's put our heads together and resume
what we both know to be a lie in fact
our sad relationship: - and yet at that
not all unreal but getting fairly urgent
because at last the news is out Miz Moon
you time is up & you are coming back
and some are ready here and waiting
come in my love the window's open
& each black fish that swims the ocean
may curl upon your own moonlit neck
Friends can't you hear her? Buvons á Zelda
Miz Moon is climbing up the stairs
& life itself is turning dangerous
though Christ alone knows how we've wasted
& spent the night-times riding sleepers
for fear of being the next day's wreck
but let us get this in perspective
word is Miz Moon you're coming back
& we will have a blitzed-out evening
which will not please the Doctors but
our inner organs peeled and then some
Miz Moon you're home and welcome

HOUSERULES

Hoop-la said my working wife
this woman says there were two kinds of amazons
(and she looked at me over her tee ell ess)
the ones who went in for househusbands
and the others... random copulators
who only hit the ground in spots

Measuring-up to my responsibilities
I called to my wife starting out for work
could you take my head in to town today please
have my hair cut and my beard trimmed
for this poetry reading on Thursday
(I was dusting my high-heeled Spanish boots)

Gladly: she threw the talking head
in the back of the car with her lecture notes
her handbag fur coat and galley proofs
tricks of trade and mercantile accoutrements
Otrivine stuffed firmly up my nostrils
to stop catarrh and Hacks for my throat

Leaving me headless and in some straits:
considering the ways of well set-up amazons
as I fumbled helplessly around the garden
playing blind man's buff to a dancing clothesline
stubbing my pegs on air and thinking with envy
of my neighbour and his empire of cabbages

DAYS OF MAY 1985
(for Niall)

In the village street a stained-glass artist
Is trawling the shops for Brunswick black
On a morning when my mind is taken up with light
And light effects on silver halides

Or in Russells on a bleary Wednesday
Clients push in chafing and shooting their cuffs
Signalling pints but 'spirits out first please'
Such are the limits of a year's horizons

This week brought Paul Durcan's postcard
With news of Robert Frost and mention of Mt.
LaFayette
A catalogue of timber in New Hampshire
And yesterday my wife sailed in from Paris

To find me dressed again in campaign summer gear
Which doesn't differ much in truth from winter's
The addition or the stripping of a layer plus
decorations
For my regimental Thursdays in the mad house

Being thus strappadoed I must have my story straight
And in my ley-lines find a bill of credence
Pick up on Leeson Street where I was born -
In the Appian Way my bones of childhood mock me

Yet these May mornings toiling to the Nursery
I sense my father's ghost in the wheeling migrant birds
And soon I can accept the electric invitation
Of my amazing son to the breathless world of cherry
flowers.

STOPPING THE LIGHTS, RANELAGH 1986
(for Niall)

1.

Two hands to the bottle of Wincarnis
this timeless gent his cap turned back to front
arranges himself in the delta of downtown Ranelagh
and sits on the public bench first
carefully hitching his trousers at the knee
preserving the delicate break over the instep
advised by Bertie Wooster's Jeeves
he hefts the bottle up and sucking deep
with one eye shut he draws a bead

Secure in his well constructed tree top hide
Lord Graystokes fixes on the jungle
in between the changing of the traffic lights
like drops of blood the amber jewels of his rood
accurately lights a cigarette
The lion - he mouths - *The lion sleeps tonight*
The traffic beacons change
controlled and manageable their peacock march
from green to red and red to green
Ring out wild bells: he settles back

A businesslike nun swims into frame
intervenes in a pale cold car behold
and disengaging gear
reflects a while in Gordon's hardware shop
the glass of her aquarium is hung
with buses plastic basins toasters
electric kettles lengths of timber super-glue
bronze fire-dogs brooms and Bilton dinner-sets
here on the veldt
she brings a missionary whisper
the folded mysteries of convent breakfasts
white linen and starched altar cloths
white cattle birds half glimsed in Africa

lights flash cars slip into gear slide off

And the delta has become my launching pad
my swampland Florida
junkyard of burnt out rocket systems
where all that thrust falls back to earth
to rust in secret in the Corporation Park
my blue-eyed son is friend to man
and guides me through the shadowy tangled paths
where alligators twine and lurk
and I learn to recognise my lunar neighbours
among mysterious constellations

2.

It takes some time to make an epic
or to see it for the epic that it is
an eighteenth century balloonist
when Mars was in the Sun set out for Wales from here
trailing sparks ascended through the clouds
and sank to earth near Howth
while dancing masters in the Pleasure Gardens
played musical glasses in the undergrowth
they have used the story to rename a pub
to make a Richard Crosbie of the Chariot and

We too have come through dangers and we call
to the MC on the console *stop the lights*
here at the wrong end of the telescope
my one concern is holding down the present
Sunday mornings on the Great South Wall are real
and hand in hand with Niall it is enough
when we are astral travellers and our astral turf
the cut blocks that interlock upon each other
and we are inaccessible and far off dots
on the Half Moon road to the lighthouse
safe from the law alive and well
in the wind on the Great South Wall.

SANTA MARIA NOVELLA

This lonely angular man in railway stations
going home by cloud or wherever and travelling
                                    collapso
in the polish of Santa Maria Novella
drinking an orange juice and smoking a gauloise
he pauses mid-journey poised and folded at his table
warily by times and almost paternal
he eyes his Gucci-type metal executive briefcase
his sorcerer's link with home and substance
as if he has just been told it contains a time bomb
and his time has ticked its hour up

Nor is he any too sure of these foreign coins
and he lays them out on his palm at intervals
to inspect them and survey them into sense
and all unbeknownst to him his eyebrows creep up
his head twitches to the side and his eyes widen
as he talks to the coins giving them instruction
and his other angular hand unships itself
an admonitory digit wagging up and down
until it anchors in under his chin
and he returns to the station self-service Ristorante
wondering if we have noticed his temporary absence

But we are all at odds here quartered off
set apart behind a bright green rope

I am considering the kilo of garlic in my bag
its oils and its fine rich weight and aroma
and this Florentine heat and I'm wondering
if my fellow passengers on the night train to Paris
will appreciate my addition to their journey
and all unbeknownst to myself
I have lifted the plastic bag to my head inhaling

as if to clear a lifetime of asthma
bursting my lungs with the must of garlic
I am tunnelling beneath the platforms of Florence
fiercely with my eyes shut
crushing wild garlic on the walls of my sett

Among the reflections and marble of Santa Maria
                                            Novella
magic samurai are sheathing magic cameras
a waiter slides by on velvet skates
an elderly German hitches up his shorts
the cool service area pauses unexpectantly
- again nothing has happened -
and the catch of the station clock flips over

ANGELICA SAVED BY RUGGIERO

This girl I recognise her
from the filleting room at the back of Keegan's
dismembering North Sea haddock saithe and spur-dog
now at nine o'clock in the morning
I watch her striding through the dry-ice air
red hair the colour of insides of sea-urchins
herself like an underwater creature
she flits and darts through the morning traffic
wrapped around in her red and white stripes
to the shade and shell of her souk

I caught her in a net and brought her home one night
as befits me a convicted anarchist
who himself keeps a roadside stall in Tripoli
not far from the Azizia barracks
a thousand miles east of the Rue Bab Rob
one month's journey through the territory of ostriches
a two month journey travelling by ostrich
subsisting only on their chalky eggs

I seized her like a myth and brought her home
to this courtyard market and charnel shambles
my carpeted rooms up under the roof
sat her on the floor and to protect her from the night
wrapped her in a kefia from Damascus
gave her a gold-work kaftan and slippers for her feet
filled glasses of mahia from Marrakesh
served mejoun and mint tea on an inlaid table
and coffee taken from the heat three times
thick black coffee from Cairo

And up beneath the slippery roof
we skewered fish kebabs and prawns for a feast
clams caught that morning in Essouira
while we gazed out through the windows at the sky
past Rats' Castle and the old men's home

beyond the Burlington to the mouth of the river
suspended in the silver nitrate moon
and the minarets of the Pigeon House
until I saw her deep-sea eyes cloud up

This happens in mid-sentence
with our finger on the page we lose our place
delaying we were caught between the tides
while the foreshore lengthened all around
into a dim anonymous suburban pub
with the elements and furniture of sea-wrack
rising up from the floor to claim us
ash-trays and razor-shells a palm-court pianist
and in the corner hung with sea-weed
a supermarket trolley rusting in the sand

The level sands stretched out and that was it
new myths spring up beneath each step we take
always another fact or proposition missed
and just for a moment we almost touched
though she knows nothing of it now in cold December
dancing out of the Ingres painting
and making her way down the morning street
she pauses in mid-stride then looks away
freed from that scenario of chain and rock
Andromeda - this girl -I recognise her

AFTER THE SLANE CONCERT

The dark girl drinking cider in the bar
smiles speaking of her knife
my ears prick at the hint of violence
with thoughts of a dark street in Paris
almost thirty years ago
stoned high and fighting with a one-eyed Arab
above that Metro shelter
the quick flash of violence and sex
and short knives stabbing across the street

He was pissing sideways says the girl
like he wasn't aiming straight
and... and here her voice drops out of sight
her hair mingles with her neighbour's
like curtains falling across the street
I think of Borges' Argentinians
dying in limelight under street lamps
it is all so casual so promiscuous
so soft these lethal beautiful parishioners

And was it really just like this -
an inner city pub where careless Fates
blast on cider and cigarettes
so sure-footed and so self-contained
one smiling danger but as innocent of violence
as the knife-blade in its hidden place
- and one maimed look is all it needs
to make us human
reading in the morning ash for messages of love?

Bastille Day 1987

54

SECONDS OUT

After Humpty Dumpty fell apart
they said they would reconstitute him
in the Seconds-Factory
iron out the folds in his carapace
rebuild him with sellotape and cowgum
three square meals a day
and some confrontation therapy

It would be hard they said
a stiff course for an egg
- an egg who suspected he'd be better off
robbing mail trains
or turning tricks on the canal bank -
a stiff course for an egg
but they would make a man of him

As in the end they did
a man of weights and measures
stripping five thousand crocus flowers
to procure an ounce of saffron:
in Cambodia there is no more gamboge yellow
and at the speed of light
sons are older than their space-men fathers

IN THE RANELAGH GARDENS:
EASTER SATURDAY 1988

Easter falls early this year
at the end of a mild winter -
tomorrow the sun will dance on the ceiling
at midnight on Thursday by the sea I heard
Summer rustling in the palms

Listen said the voice
for years I have been fighting my way up out of this
climbing out of this black hole
pushing past the bog oak
and this black weight that hugs my rib cage

On a street corner in Rome my brother-in-law
the Guardian of Paradise reflects
Arabian gentleman in camel hair
how can I have grown so old he says
staring into his daughter's camera lens

I thought of him again last night
and looked for patterns in our ad hoc lives
breathing cool air from the surface of the pond
remembering I must not be in competition
not even with myself

Listen said the voice
for years I have been in the shallows of this lake
a creature of the reeds
hunting under drowned and folded leaves
with the water beetles

JOHN F. DEANE

FACING NORTH
(Isaiah 1:6)

It is little to do with me, I thought, waiting.

"Flight EI 607 to London:
will passengers please board through gate no. 9"

So I followed her tall full body down the corridor
clutching the buttocks soft as ocean swell beneath tight
jeans,
my teeth bit off the bra that whispered through her
blouse,
chewed her high nipples; tongue moved down
lingeringly between the fragrant rhythmic thighs,
soul drowned among the ripples of her hair.

In furtive London streets my Irish stride
shattered the plate glass, rubbled the marble buildings;
a whore in Soho spurned me for my speech.

"Flight EI 706 to Dublin:
passengers now boarding through gate no. 9"

So I followed her tall full body down the corridor;
from the sole of her foot even to her head
there was no soundness in her, suppurating
bruises, sores and wounds. My hands are full of blood.

ISLAND WOMAN

It wasn't just the building of a bridge,
for even before, they had gone by sea
to Westport and from there abroad, and each
child sent money home till death in the family
brought him, reluctant, back. Of course the island
grew rich and hard, looked, they say, like Cleveland.

On a bridge the traffic moves both ways.
My own sons went and came, their sons, and theirs.
Each time, in the empty dawn, I used to pray
and I still do, for mothers. I was there
when the last great eagle fell in a ditch.
My breasts are warts. I never crossed the bridge.

MATINS

We walked round shrubbery, cowled in silence,
somewhere in the long pause of mid-morning;
the fuchsia hung in scarlet, bees drew out
their honey; high trees benignly watched, long
used to circling figures on the gravel; we
read Rodriguez, his tome of huge wonders, deeds
of saints, glories of holiness, miracles
sprouting out of deserts. Secretly, I longed
that those naked whores spirited out of hell
into the monks' cells should tempt me, too;
I fasted, prayed, scaled the cliffs of sanctity
to no avail; always the sudden wren
distracted, a weed's unexpected beauty on a stone,
coolness of peas bursting against my palette; I
stayed in my tiny group, going round and round.

ON A DARK NIGHT

On a dark night
When all the street was hushed, you crept
Out of our bed and down the carpeted stair.
I stirred, unknowing that some light
Within you had gone out, and still I slept.
As if, out of the dark air

Of night, some call
Drew you, you moved in the silent street
Where cars were white in frost. Beyond the gate
You were your shadow on a garage-wall.
Mud on our laneway touched your naked feet.
The dying elms of our estate

Became your bower
And on your neck the chilling airs
Moved freely. I was not there when you kept
Such a hopeless tryst. At this most silent hour
You walked distracted with your heavy cares
On a dark night while I slept.

CORAL STRAND

I see your figure stooping on the sand
in winter cold, with the wild sea
behind you, you are held in the history
of shells - cowrie, periwinkle, whelk -
in their white disintegration on the strand;

how could I, loving you, imagine then
your dying, where I stood on rocks at the shore
of your mystery? Now, on a train I pass
over a causeway where men have been channeling
tides; from our flanged hurrying the shorebirds -

shell-duck, oystercatcher, gull - shear
away; I see them in their countless generations
stab at living things on the shore
of a changeless ocean; my face, perplexed,
is staring back at me from the window.

WINTER IN MEATH
(to Tomas Tranströmer)

again we have been surprised
deprived, as if suddenly,
of the earth's familiarity

it is like the snatching away of love
making you aware at last you loved

sorrows force their way in, and pain
like memories half contained

the small birds, testing boldness, leave
delicate tracks
                closer
to the back door

while the cherry flaunts blossoms of frost
and stands in desperate isolation

the base of the hedgerow is a cliff of snow
the field is a still of a choppy sea
white waves capped in a green spray

a grave was dug into that hard soil
and overnight the mound of earth
grew stiff and white as stones flung onto a beach

our midday ceremony was hurried, forced
hyacinths and holly wreathes dream birds
appearing on our horizonless ocean

the body sank slowly
the sea closed over
things on the seabed stirred
again in expectation

this is a terrible desolation

the word 'forever'
stilling all the air

to glass

night tosses and seethes;
mind and body chafed all day
as a mussel-boat restlessly irritates
the mooring

on estuary water a fisherman
drags a long rake against the tide; one
snap of a rope and boat and this
solitary man
sweep off together into night

perhaps the light from my window
will register a moment with some god
riding by on infrangible glory

at dawn
names of the dead
appear on the pane
                    beautiful
in undecipherable frost

breath
hurts them
and they fade

the sea has gone grey as the sky

and as violent

pier and jetty go under
again and again
as a people suffering losses

a flock of teal from the world's edge
moves low over the water
finding grip for their wings along the wind

already among stones
a man
        like a priest
stooping in black clothes
has begun beachcombing

the dead, gone silent in their graves
have learned the truth about resurrection

you can almost look into the sun
silver in its silver-blue monstrance
cold over the barren white cloth of the world

for nothing happens

each day is an endless waiting
for the freezing endlessness of the dark

once - as if you had come across
a photograph, or a scarf maybe - a silver
monoplane like a knife-blade cut
across the still and haughty sky

but the sky healed up again after the passing that left
only a faint, pink thread, like a scar

PHOTOGRAPH
(25 January 1945)

though released you return
make invisible circles about me;
black, and white, and your child's wild hair;
as a bird that is held by the merest thread
you are near me; cardboard has curled

as your child's wild hair;
those eyes, that smile, before they are dead
must absorb years of pain; curtains fade
in the background, as ghosts that are caught
attempting to escape through the walls

at death's unexpected snap;
black, and white, and your child's wild hair,
as if hot summer winds were blowing, is fair;
but the table is solid, and the dust of use
greys the soles of your shoes, they forgot

dust on the soles of your shoes;
black, and white, and your child's wild hair
carefully tossed; your gaze is so lightly
focused beyond us - or could you foresee
your soul make invisible circles about me?

FRANCIS OF ASSISI 1182 : 1982

Summer has settled in again; ships,
softened to clouds, hang on the horizon;
buttercups, like bubbles, float
on fields of a silver-grey haze;
words recur, such as light, the sea, and God;

the frenzy of crowds jostling towards the sun
contains silence, as eyes
contain blindness; we say, may the Lord
turning his face towards you
give you peace;

morning and afternoon the cars moved out
onto the beach and clustered, shimmering,
as silver herring do in a raised net;
this is a raucous canticle to the sun.

Altissimu, omnipotente, bon Signore...

To set up flesh
in images of snow and of white roses,
to preach to the sea on silence,
to man on love,
is to strain towards death
as towards a body without flaw;

our poems, too, are gestures of a faith
that words of an undying love
may not be without some substance;

words hovered like larks about his head,
dropped like blood from his ruptured hands.

tue so'le laude, et onne benedictione...

We play, like children, awed and hesitant
at the ocean's edge;
between dusk and dark the sea
as if it were God's long and reaching fingers
appropriates each footprint from the sand;

I write down words, such as light, the sea, and God
and a bell rides out across the fields
like a man on a horse with helmet and lance
gesturing foolishly towards night.

laudato si, Signore,
per sora nostra morte corporale...

At night, cars project
ballets of brightness and shadow on the trees
and pass, pursuing darkness
at the end of their tunnels of light;

the restful voices have been swept by time
beyond that storybook night sky
where silence
drowns them out totally.

DELIKAT-ESSEN

At the far right of the superstore
    the meats garden - discreet lighting,
hallucinatory waterfalls;
    only progressive democrats shop here,
feeding off lives
    crushed under the belly of history;

neat rows of quail, all trussed and dainty
    like young girls' breasts;
rabbits, hares, caught in flight and skinned,
    laid out nude, purpling, like babies;
chops, here, have been dressed in frilly socks;
    on trays, as if a Salome had passed,

are livers, kidneys, hearts, and tongues.
    Among these clasically landscaped meatbeds -
low hedges of parsley sprigs,
    cress, sculpted tomato busts -
you will find the names absent from history.
    Oh to stand on a wooden Chiquita banana box

and urge theologies of liberation!
    but all who come
nod to the government officials in their white coats,
    machetes, bone-saws in their holsters,
      and blood - like maps of Uruguay, Guatemala and
                                 Peru -
staining their elegant tuxedoes.

AMETHYST

A young priest, eager, with white hair, and a boy
scaling the mountain; intoxicating heat
hangs above them; they are high and sweat
in the mercy of a violet sky.

In a mountain pool, among heather canopies,
they are naked; the boy's white body; and his fear
as if a hawk had suddenly stooped near
shadowing him. The stone, kept, for its silences.

THE HARROWING OF HELL

Days of hushed waiting; the man
after long suffering, waits, a glazed
fragility about him; cars stuttering
over cattlegrids, the undertaker's

bustle, will release new life, words
and tears; the naked dead, with bright
alabaster faces, led meekly out
into impenetrable light.

SUNFLOWERS

Earth-coloured people, potato eaters,
we too look up, expecting
new colours in the sky;

gravestones in the churchyard
already taunt us, flaunting our names
where dandelion tubers grow
big as fists. The man

who gave his canvasses
as clothing for the poor, had hoped, like us,
for brighter colours
and had filled the world with sunflowers,
gifts of yellow light, simplicities,
like Japanese prints, deft
individual strokes of paint for bridge
or tree or man.

But night threatened; his hatband
was a bush of lighting candles;
he tried to cry, but no tears came;
he painted a field
coloured like angry sunflowers where crows
were gathering, where earth-coloured paths
led suddenly off the canvas;

his yellows grew too hot
and the sky filled with a black rain;

if you were to take a gun now
against those crows before the violent mistral
dries your brain to ice,
ending the Japanese dream,
Hiroshima, Nagasaki,
earth-coloured people, who tried to cry...

CYCLE

Now, among familiar gulls and curlews
on the sand banks offshore -
the winter birds: bright memories,

their seasoning, infiltration, term.
The teal, bath-duck, compact exotic corporal;
the grey-lag, goose, ashen, dull,

a tawdry follower, fag-end.
Achill was home, birds coming low at dusk
over chill acres, strewn out

like words on a darkening page;
among the reed-beds rifle shots
made evening livid with their shattered sentences.

She, out of these deaths, took wings
for dusters, the curved knuckle,
the bracing of quills, the patient

sshhh of the feathers. Today they float,
ringed foreigners, on Dublin bay
and she homes low towards death,

words scattered like dust about her.
Call out: and wings in flight make a moaning sound,
the effort of limbs pounding the air in panic.

REMEMBRANCE DAY

Behind the statue of St. Teresa of the Flowers
a brown package, the message, the ransom note.
Somewhere a room where men in balaclavas

play at dice; safe houses. Rose petals
fall on us from the clouds. A soldier
broods over the named and the unnamed dead

of another war, the cenotaph, the empty tomb.
The gable end of a street
has swollen out like a balloon; our prayers

are pinned like poppies into our lapels.
Our arms have been growing into wreathes.
In the quiet of the night we go on crying, very hard.

*

After the bombardment apple-blossom fell
like snow in Normandy; retreating soldiers pushed
through Caen towards Paris. Under rubble of her town

the little saint lay undisturbed; I choose,
she had said, everything, her arms folded,
her eyes held down, turning and turning

in the chestnut-tree walk of her convent grounds,
the sky above her full of leaves, like prayers;
someone comes, with wheelbarrow and rake, and
                                                      works

among the shadows of the trees. When they clothed
                                                      her
snow fell on her garden, and the chestnut-trees
were apple orchards blossoming.

SISTER MOTHER EARTH

Summer in Umbria; the light demanding,
hill-top villages safe inside their walls;

there are meadows filled with sunflowers,
ranks of vines stand mute before their god;

Umbria's holy men
journeying from dream to dream

denounced cupidity;
their conversations not of this world

they walked on air, from their dark cells
willing their lives to float

into the mothering arms of God.

*

She stood, spongeing her breasts,
the frightening hair in her armpits,
and watched me watching her;

she would pray O Lord
lead my soul out from the prison of its flesh.
Once a pheasant rose startled out of scutch grass;

it flew towards reflected sky
and cracked its back against the living-room window;
I touched warm feathers, but the eyes were dulled.

Rhubarb and gooseberries
thrive in our sunless garden;
near us a house,

chicken-shit on flag and hearth and window-ledge;
there was a child, small and yellow,
you could see the small and yellow hang of his testicles

through rips in his canvas pants;
I was sent to buy eggs, and I grew terrified
of the snapping dog, the darkness,

the lean old woman's cackling banter.

*

Summer in Umbria; over the glowing towns
the swifts are tiny flecks

darting on the retina of the sky;
and only he

could summon them to stillness
while he told the villagers of God. Francis

had been elegant, dainty, debonair;
now he begged Lord cast your light

into the darkness of my heart.
Perhaps the wolf of Gubbio

is the rage of death in the flesh,
and little sister hare

the frightened dashes of love before the hounds.
Too much gazing towards the sun

brings blindness,
too great a pity brings a gash into the side

and sores onto the hands and feet.

*

At night, in the room upstairs, I prayed
O angel of God my guardian...
Mother's voice was a distant murmuring,

I had a dread of presences in the dark,
of shapes of devils that might yet emerge
from round the curtain's edge. Now I fear

blindness, when sometimes words
blur on a page, and sometimes
yellow streetlamps smudge; Lord

cast your light into the darkness of my heart.

*

Once I cupped a swift, young, abandoned,
in the nest of my hand;

I felt the heart beat rhythmically against my palm,
the tiny noughts of its eyes were points of unknowing,

its soot-soft feathers warm, its small body trembling;
I held it high and let it go; it flopped

and groped, ungainly, back onto my hand;
time and again I freed it until at last it flew,

its dip and glide a triumph, a farewell.

*

When he went blind they laid white-hot iron bars
against his temples and he cried out praise to God;

today, in the cloisters of Assisi
a white dove nests in the stone palms of the saint.

Somewhere between the drag of flesh
and the hope of resurrection my poems happen;

it is said his bones never crumbled into earth,
I came to see the holes that the nails made,

to put my hand into his side,
but he, too, is locked from sight in a stone box

and Umbria's holy men are ranged about him.

*

I helped her into bed and held her hand a while;
she was thin, bird-limbed, and her eyes dulled.
She watched me watching her, and could not name
me.

Soon she will be released, like a sigh,
into the air. I left; there was a pale
blue night-light in the darkness of her room.

THE MUSEUM OF COSMONAUTICS

They took the Church of the Sacred Martyrs
and made of it the Museum of Farm Implements;

the meringues of the cupolas they hollowed out:

like taking someone's head
and spooning out the memories to leave it
clean as the shell of an egg.

On Prospect Mira - the Avenue of Peace -
an obelisk of titanium and steel
is the Museum of Space Machinery;

an old lady, with authority, insists we wear
huge museum-slippers within the stylobate;
snow-shoes, pumps, we are too small for our boots.

Russia has been to the stars and back;
here are the diagrams, the charts,
bell-jars, peppercanisters and the squared
gleaming spiders that have probed the skull of space;

we flop about in admiration,
clenching our toes to keep our feet on the ground.

Outside it is cold;
there is a man who wants to give us roubles
for our pounds; the Russians
have splendid coats and furs, they know
there is nothing on the far side of the moon.

LOVE-POEM: LEITRIM

A spattering of sloes against the sky;
stars sharp as thorns and as sudden;
over the valley's crotch a witch's shark-tooth moon;

I hear the cracking of littlest bones
between the jaws of night predators,
whose unseen, watching eyes are insolent, and round.

A blue flush on the sloe's skin
comes away with the touch of a finger;
sometimes, after love, I lay my head
quietly on the hills of her breasts

dreading cold that will enter limbs
with a sound as of glass shattering,
and the angel's lifted finger
singling me out, berry, frost-petal, skull.

PADRAIG J. DALY

EVENING AT OSTIA
(In memory of Pier Paolo Pasolini)

When evening came, the red flowers were watered
On the balconies; the air was heavy with their scent.
The overflow dripped softly to the pavings, like
                                            rainfall.
People came out now to walk in the coolness.

Tablecloths were spread outside the trattorie;
Under a stark white bulb, a man sold triangles of
                                            melon;
Microphones blared songs of tenderness from a circus
                                            tent;
Lions jumped, seals went through hoops, horses
galloped on the sawdust.

The wineshops were open well into dark.
You could still smell the long flitches
Of the morning's bread. Someone argued far above;
Through a window, a new Caruso was singing.

There were notices forbidding people onto the pier.
Fishermen and lovers climbed, laughing,
Past the barriers; the sea itself
Was feverish and warm.

Cars sped by with their midnight revellers.
Brakes screeched at every crossing;
The crowds had gathered to where the light was,
The deckchairs were all folded, the sand raked clean.

So if he cried out, from this his last wilderness,
There was no one to hear.

HOUSES OFF FRANCIS STREET

I have been four years away
From an Irish Autumn
And had almost quite forgotten
How trees suddenly turn gold
And drop their beauty
Spendthrift to earth.

I had almost forgotten
The slanting passages
The sunlight makes through
The woods at eveningtime,
Clouds shapechanging
Continually, fields glowing orange.

I had forgotten too how
The houses off Francis Street
Cling for warmth together
Just as twilight comes
And the quiet smoke begins
To hide them from the stars.

LORD AND MASTER

You need have no worry about love.
It will mean what you wish it to mean.
No more. You are lord and master of your life.

Nevertheless you will lie awake
After your fullest days thinking
Of the winds crossing the shallow
Waterponds in the fields after rain
And wet hayricks tied with stones.

And sometimes a bird will fly
Across your courtyard out of the dark
Carrying a question;
Regard it simply as a stratagem
Of the God you cannot prove.
Have the porter say you're out.

PROBLEM

I understand Francis - all the stuff about the birds,
Throwing his clothes at his father; the singing, praising
                                                    heart.

Once I travelled from Rome into Umbria
To his towns, his green mountains,
His fast streams,

Saw the coarse cloth he wore against cold,
The chapel shrining Chiara's hair.

Teresa Sanchez was never a problem:
In convent or covered wagon
In constant seesaw up and down towards God.

Or John
Soaring through his bars like a linnet in song.

But I am blind still to the Jew
My life traipses after;

And the spacelessness of God
Hesitates the hand I reach
Behind cross and tabernacle
Into his paltry loneliness.

AUGUSTINE: LETTER TO GOD

1

Where praise is impossible
I will praise;
And sing where sound faces silence.

I carry death about in me
And inevitable
Cold;

Yet I will sing
Or, failing,
Burst asunder with love.

2

Man cannot evade You:
Every wary mouse,
The ant that builds and climbs,

Each small limpet on a rock,
The waters sucked noisily
Through stones on the shore,

The sleek and watery cormorant
Compel him
To shout You out.

He is the phosphorus sea
Stirred to consciousness,
The cold gravels of the underbed.

From the acids of first time,
From the tepid waters of creation
He draws his voice;

And all creation -
Beating at his flesh and pores,
Binds him to praise.

And all creation -
Hills rising out of him
Into sudden seas,

Black shoreline,
The ocean's grit -
Binds him inescapably to praise.

And nowhere but in praise
Can quark or atom
Or any fraction else of mass

Find peace.

3

Each flower
Requires knowledge

And the raindrops
On the curlew's wing

Fall
As questions.

There is a curiosity
In every piece of burnt wood.

4

What am I
That You require me?

And what is my house
That You should come to it?

And what my love that
You demand my loving

And I am lost
Unless I reach and love?

5

I call:
And You are already in my voice.

I stretch:
And You are trembling at my fingertips.

You are here and smiling
While I send invitations out.

I draw circles to contain You,
Make clay jars:

But You are
Circle and jar

And the space within
And the space without

And the spacelessness
Without the final space,

Place
Where place has no meaning,

Time
Where all is an endless now.

I call
And I am my own answer;

I stretch
Only to where I have started.

DOLLYMOUNT

Today was a bright day of Winter,
A gold rim had broken
Out upon the edges of the clouds:

There was a dog before me
Running for a stick,
A crow picking a white bone,

Three boys climbing the sandhills,
Dunlins playing games of chiaroscuro
With the day.

I walked against the wind and sunlight blindly,
My heart still clouded
By your gloom.

I wish my love could fold you
Away from your dark
To this intenseness of day.

I touch, I hold you to me,
For my own poor comforting,
My love enfeebling what it loves.

Lord, across these waters freely
Let my heart float
To bright islands.

DIOCLETIAN'S PALACE, SPLIT

Behind us, the boat rose,
All light,
Out of the water;
It had brought us
From blinding morning to sudden dusk
And looming islands in luminous seas.

The emperor of the world,
Weary of war and dusty Rome,
The long campaigns of wintertime,
Built his palace here
Like a great sculpted cliffside
Rearing from the ocean:

The water rising to his walls,
The sea halting at his doorway:
A world of tide beyond,
Fish eternally moving,
Mussels opening and closing
With the lift of ocean.

The lapping of the waters
Would set silent pace for his mind:
His prayer now, the rain's touch
On the sea;
His only battle god,
The stirring ocean.

JOURNEY

Day after day
The caravans move through the hot sun
To the clay-walled city:

The walls rise suddenly where the desert ends,
Sharp shapes cut out of sun and shadow;

Animal after animal,
huge relentless camels,
The children in light dresses running to keep pace.

These people have crossed treacherous passes and
have lived;
They have followed rockstrewn roads
By steep cliff-faces.

They have lost animals to rain and thunderstorm
When the hard mountain floated like a torrent under
them.

Here and there where grass is lushest
They make camp,
Sit at fires by night singing,
Prepare bread for their journey.

But always they must move;
And still they move:

If a man grows old among them
And the paths are steep and the ways impassible,
He will sit in some barren place
and sing himself calmly into death.

But always the caravans go onward.;
Here at the gate there is laughter,
The women chatter,

95

There will be trading for flour and cloth;

They will salute old friends,
Exchange beads and trinkets;
A marriage will be celebrated into the long starry
                                             night-time.

But at the end, at every end,
They must go onward
As if ahead somewhere were destination;

And somewhere stillness.

ENCOUNTER

Monotony of sun
On sand and scrub,
A place of wild beasts
And long shadows:

At last he comes
To green and olivegroves,
Vineyards,
Houses climbing beyond walls
Along a hillside.

Here the tempter waits,
Full of candour,
Offering for easy sale
All the green kingdoms of the world.

And he,
Though gaunt from fasting,
Needing rest,

Some perfect star
Seen a lifetime back
Determining him,

Passes slowly by.

ELEGY AT MORNINGTON

There are a few houses near the church,
Smoke comes from chimneys;

Here is quiet countryside,
Flat and undisturbed
Since the first voyagers.

Beyond the church
Old gravestones stand out against the sky.

Out there the estuary,
A causeway to the tide,
Vast mudspaces, seabirds;

A curlew is calling your name.

This morning the church was cold;
I knelt silently to remember you.

From nowhere
Gold light began to flood through windows,

Sparking the brass candlesticks,
Cutting the altarcloth in two,

Lighting the virgin in her niche,
Following the bright grains of the wood.

In its liberality,
I make it your parable.

There is always something happening
Along the estuary:

Seeping of water,
Yellow flowers opening,
Birds descending in noisy flocks,

Appearing, disappearing,
Making figures of eight in the sky;

And youngsters always
Searching for something beautiful and strange.

You called your daughter Catherine,
Your happiness at her birth
A blazing, circling wheel of praise.

Nowadays she begins to walk;
She has taken over your smile,
Your sudden laughter;

And in the summer light
I watch her clap her hands at songbirds
With your same wonder.

In the flat lands beyond your house
Swans call across the air,

The sands have covered over
The ruins of limestone castles.

Your house is sheltered by tall trees,
Your kitchen door opens onto meadows;
Horses in the distance race through yellow fields.

And nowadays your husband, for your sake,
Tends the desert of your garden
Into abundant fruitfulness.

NOVITIATE

Christmas was the start of our disillusion:
Advent was full of light and promises and stars.
At Christmas we expected the world to explode
So full was was all the earth of expectation
And justice to pour down like rain out of the skies.

We found ourselves that afternoon by the french
windows
Looking down on the city,
Excluded from familiar warmth
Like Joseph seeking room in Bethlehem.

DEATH
(After the Irish)

And must I leave this world of music,
Of fine clothes and feathered couch,
And after all my years of plenty
Loose my boat on the empty seas?

Must I leave my house behind,
My name with my friends,
The food on my tables, the golden cups,
For a currach made of sticks
And the cold sky?

I fear the wrecking of the waves,
The tearing of flesh from bone,
My body tossed like a cork on the tide,
Thrown on some far island,
Dragging a track along the sands.

I fear my little boat will sink without trace
When the tempests come:

O Christ be near, O Christ, and pity me.

EMBARQUEMENT

You must walk over the mud
To reach the boat:

There are miles of emptiness to cross
Before you come to the channel
Where the river goes to sea.

Sometimes the mud is to your knees;
Seagulls will annoy you
With their hostile calling;

You must go over green slime
And keep your feet.

(If it rains, delay your journey).

You climb thick ropes to the hold,
The boat lists to its side.

Persevere!
In the evening
Great swelling of water will carry you.

TWO PAINTINGS BY SIDNEY NOLAN

1. AFTER GLENROWAN SIEGE

Ned wounded Kelly in his tin hat,
Full of all the pain of our poverty and our Irishness,
A red blob where his eye should be.

Torn curtains like rags at a well,
Smell of smoke and burning,
A wooden stake through the heart of the world.

2. KELLY'S SPRING

Ned Kelly's Easter:
Flowers blossoming above his tinpot head,
Everything coming alive and glimmering,
The world in song.

SHADOWS

I have come indoors again to shadow:
Shadows of the wind stirring the leaves on the trees,
Shadows of gateposts and gables
Leaping or failing with the leap and the failure of light,
Red and ochre shadow through walls of glass.

Plato thought that all this shining world that we
                                        admire
Was a shadow of what was real.
I am happy however among such shadows;
And my heaven is a sunlit city
With flowers in tubs and water falling
And the radiant company of the dead.

THOMAS MERTON

What is to be said about silence
Except that it is;
And you sought it out diligently in your woods,
Living alone with your books,
In the company of birds;

Walking to morning prayer on a snow carpet,
Nothing there before you
But the marks of the monastery cat
On the white ground;

Or the form where deer slept
Close to your window,
Rhythmically heaving with your sleep's heaving?

And there is little you can send us out of your silence
Except to say that it is;
And it cries out louder than our clamour.

STOP

Sometimes we stop on the journey
As once at evening by mountain guarded seas,
White swans moving to us on luminous waters,
Full of immortal promise;
Or reaching after long months a turretted city,
Carried outside ourselves by singing stone.

Afterwards the journey continues:
We plod again through desert,
Eyes blinded by blowing sands,
Minds fixed on clay and the works of clay.

INTRUDER

You came from that early time
Before I began to lay my garden out
With its lawns and rockeries and wroughtiron chairs;
Plots of thyme, lupin, marigold,
Broom grown from seed gathered one Autumn on a
                                                  slope outside Rome.

Meditative swans glided among the lilies,
Peacocks like dandies strode the lawn,
The country birds made nests in the hedges.
I planted nettles too to draw coloured butterflies
And purple stock to scent the twilight air.

I had happily banished you and all the time of your
                                                              cruelty,
When you came, full of smiles,
As if we had been together days before,
Trampling as you walked
All my glorious borders.

LISIEUX

At one corner of the courtyard
They grew nettles,
Lush and cruel
As the giants of their most fretful sleep.

The older women took them to their beds
In pious atonement of their faults.

Thérèse had penance enough in broken waterjugs,
A nun clicking her teeth as she prayed,
All the agony of constant closeness;

And in her room at night,
She shivered at the thought of God growing strange;
And a death as final as the death of stars.

MILAN

First there was a brown wall crumbling along by the
                                                    roadway;
Then a field of ripe wheat with towering heads of
                                                    thistle,
Red poppyflower.

Then a park with footballers;
And pigeons making commotion in the trees;
High apartment blocks, flowerstalls, dusty streets;

And all the people of the city
Hurrying past with urgent purpose,

Each held to each by webs of importance;
Such as save us
From plunging beneath the great wheels of buses.

DENNIS O'DRISCOLL

KIST

(i.m. 14th February 1975)

On that lovers' morning, our hearts chimed.
Later, the slow death knell of hers
and a coffin door slamming
in her last chill breath.

Preparing me for your death, then,
I noticed silver strands,
coffin-handle bright,
beneath your oak-brown hair.

And, pacing behind hearse,
my own face in its glass
took on the wrinkled grain
of coffin wood.

SIBLINGS

I am writing at exactly the moment
you had sent me the message of his death
precisely this time last year.

Returning home from school to an empty house,
you have begun to live your own lives with the
                                    vulnerability
of those who know how thin the barrier of flesh is,

that looking forward becomes looking back
until there is nothing either way but death.
It is quiet in the office as I write,

hiding this paper under a file,
heat rising from radiators, first cigarettes being lit,
someone whistling, someone listing soccer scores.

We have spent a year without him now,
his thoughts scattered, his burden of organs eased.
This is just another working day here

of queries, letters, tea-breaks, forms.
Any minute now some telephone will ring
but I do not dread its news, as then.

I concentrate upon this moment, cup it in my hands,
to understand what the shedding of his skin might
                                    signify
and what you have lost in these past years

in which home has become orphanage
and we have soiled the carpet in the hall
with the clay of their two burials,

our world refracted by a lens of tears.

SOMEONE

someone is dressing up for death today, a change of
                                        skirt or tie
eating a final feast of buttered sliced pan, tea
scarcely having noticed the erection that was his last
shaving his face to marble for the icy laying out
spraying with deodorant her coarse armpit grass
someone today is leaving home on business
saluting, terminally, the neighbours who will join in
                                        the cortége
someone is trimming his nails for the last time, a
                                        precious moment
someone's thighs will not be streaked with elastic in
                                        the future
someone is putting out milkbottles for a day that will
                                        not come
someone's fresh breath is about to be taken clean away
someone is writing a cheque that will be marked
                                        'drawer deceased'
someone is circling posthumous dates on a calendar
someone is listening to an irrelevant weather forecast
someone is making rash promises to friends
someone's coffin is being sanded, laminated, shined
who feels this morning quite as well as ever
someone if asked would find nothing remarkable in
                                        today's date
perfume and goodbyes her final will and testament
someone today is seeing the world for the last time
as innocently as he had seen it first

FIRST IMPRESSIONS

Open the hall door
and let the year's first sunlight in,
picking its way through coal seams of darkness:
a gleaming copper hot-water pipe;
a bale of wheaten straw;
a hose of light drenching our chambered mound.

Hard green supermarket pears mellow on the
                                        window-sill.
One blackbird still gives preference to our cul-de-sac.
Bedroom-pink cherry and hawthorn talc are visible
after steam baths of fog and rain,
only a powdery, eye-shadow cloud
now smudged under sun.

Bad pennies, earth's small change,
the dandelions are scattered everywhere.
Oval buds begin to hatch.
And the sun slips in through the front door,
restoring our storm-battered house,
converting it into a holiday home.

G-PLAN ANGST

He has everything.
A beautiful young wife.
A comfortable home.
A secure job.
A velvet three-piece suite.
A metallic-silver car.
A mahogany cocktail cabinet.
A rugby trophy.
A remote-controlled music centre.
A set of golf clubs under the hallstand.
A fair-haired daughter learning to walk.

What he is afraid of most
and what keeps him tossing some nights
on the electric underblanket,
listening to the antique clock
clicking as if with disapproval from the landing,
are the stories that begin:
He had everything.
A beautiful young wife.
A comfortable home.
A secure job.
Then one day.

DISTURBING MY MOTHER

It has been ten years since our last direct exchange
and I have not dared to interrupt your rest.
It is so long since we were one family,
talking together in one inviolable room.

Our silence now is like a Sunday afternoon at home
with you taking your weekly break, dozing by the fire,
the newspaper sliding down your knees,
your face palsied by twitching flames.

A decade ago your grating final breath
like a rasping gate admitted death
and we set off on our own, your offspring,
a hunted, howling, endangered flock.

On the anniversary of your assimilation into pain,
I am referred to the same hospital for an x-ray
and find another family weeping inside the door
appalled at the indifference sweeping past.

'You're finished,' the radiographer announces
and instructs me to put back my clothes and leave.
My future prospects have shown up clearly:
a ghost, free of flesh, uniting you and me.

I await the medical results as I once waited
for exam reports during tense summer holidays,
going over the symptoms in my head, like maths,
to calculate whether I pass or fail.

Everything seems possible on this Sunday morning
as sun penetrates the silence, heats the garden seat,
and a bird pumped full of song
suppresses knowledge of life's hidden extras.

Your routine of cooking, cleaning, tending, caring

ended with skin's grain invaded by malignant knots,
wheeled in an enamel dish towards the mortuary slab,
a cold meat salad smothered in a lettuce of wreaths.

WORDS FOR W.S. GRAHAM (1918-1986)

When I tap on the wall of your language,
who will be there to signal back?
What wordlouse will go scurrying between lines?

The twenty-six letters I conscript
cannot combine
to make themselves heard
above your silence.
My cursive waves break.
The water-table of language has run low.

You once wrote to say
how pleased you were
to have met me
at the Third Eye Centre in Glasgow
- where I have never been.
Address me now from where you are
- and where I have yet to see.
Speak with a sixth sense, a third eye.

Words are tonguetied by your defection.
Listen. Even the silence is silenced.
The language hides and seeks you.

WHAT SHE DOES NOT KNOW IS

That she is a widow.
That these are the last untinged memories of her life.
That he is slumped in his seat at a lay-by.
That a policeman is trying to revive him.
That the knife and fork she has set are merely
                                          decorative.
That the liver beside the pan will be left to rot.
That he has lost his appetite.
That the house she is tidying is for sale.
That the holiday photograph will be used for his
                                          memorial card.
That his sunburned body will not be subjected to direct
                                          light again.
That she will spend all night brewing tears.
That it is not his car she will soon hear slowing down
                                          outside.

STILLBORN

what we are lamenting
is what has not been
and what will not have seen
this mild May morning

what we are lamenting
is unsuckled air
and what was brought to bear
this mild May morning

what we are lamenting
is the blood and puppy fat, our child,
that has not laughed or cried
this mild May morning

what we are lamenting
is the life we crave
snatched from the cradle to the grave
this mild May morning

A LIFE STUDY

Here is a woman on a bus
half-way through a book
entitled simply *Life*.

I squint, but cannot decipher
who the author is
or what it is about.

She seems to be enjoying it
or is too absorbed at least
to look out at shoppers

wrapped up in their thoughts.
How is *Life* classified?
Fiction, allegory, myth?

Is she dying to know
the kind of ending it will have?
The book slams unexpectedly;

she gets off at the next stop.

CALF

If it is being fattened for food,
if there are people with recipes for veal
who would steal the spring from its step

or rip the stitching of its meat apart
or promote profit-growth through hormones,
the calf won't pause to contemplate such things.

If it understood words, it would not prate
about hoose, brucellosis, bovine t.b.
or the level of E.E.C. farm grants.

What it knows of the world at the moment
prompts it to run for joy, to prance,
to flap a tagged ear, swish a stippled tail.

I am reminded of it as I watch a child
with eager eyes, dainty dress, miniature rucksack,
pony-tail, hand sheltered in her mother's palm,

skipping down the street in front of me.
And I realize my own feet, dragging me to work,
have not been inspired to jump for joy in years.

SPERM

an oil slick polluting her canal
scum of humanity seed of pain

dense multiple warheads
arms racing to strike target terrain

the triumphant achieve spina bifida
or ambition malnutrition or fame

and hundreds of millions of tiny sprigs
are marketed in vain

a lost civilization
a bedclothes stain

SPOILED CHILD

my child recedes inside me
and need never puzzle where it came from
or lose a football in the dusty laurel bushes
or sneak change from my jacket to buy sweets

my child will not engage in active military service
or make excuses about its school report
or look up from a picture book, dribbling a pink smile
or qualify for free glasses or school lunch

my child will not become a prodigy of musicianship or
                                                    crime
and will evince no appetite for hamburgers or drugs
and will suffer neither orgasm nor kidney stones
reduced neither to a statistic nor a sacrifice

my child will not play space games with its cousins
or sit adrift on a grandparent's lap
or slit its wrists or erect a loving headstone on my
                                                    grave
or store a secret name for frogs or treetops

my child will not be a comfort to my old age
my child will not be cheated or promoted or denied
my child will trail me, like a guardian angel, all my life
its blemishes, its beauty, its shortcomings and its
                                                    promise

forever unsullied and unfulfilled

DEVOTIONS

1

both relished the yield
of the tree of carnal knowledge
and, like God, learned to procreate

her apple breasts enticed
stiff nipple nails sank
as they lost paradise

2

at mass you spread your tongue out
for communion
your lips lustrous with wine

I adore your wafer-pale host
that will diffuse its ether slowly
as its seal breaks

3

because beauty will not last
and time dismantles every mystery
I savour your divineness

and through your shallow skin
the stub of an angel's wing protrudes
damaged in your fall

4

in the red light of our sanctuary
a real presence is felt

the deep wound that I touch

uplifts me beyond doubt

and we kiss with a gift of tongues
and forget how Jesus was betrayed

GROWING PAINS

We have already advanced
to the stage where we can
convene seminars on cost/yield ratio
and child sexual abuse.
We have reached the point
where genetic engineering can create
a tender, tasty, waste-free sow,
a rindless cut above the rest.
It certainly is not the experts' fault
if minds, like power supplies, break down
under the strain of our pace of life
or if bodies are stifled by the human crush,
yielding tears like oil out of their rock
or if hunger sears as soils erode
- remember the humblest shanty town
is still the corrugated product
of great human skill and ingenuity.
If, rarely, a desert missile test
or rocket launch ends up in disaster,
we are capable of learning from mistakes
and will get it right the next time.
The alienated are just slow developers,
suffering the growing pains of evolution.
Out of the dung heap of chemical wastes,
a thornless mutant rose will sprout,
its scent as fragrant as a new deodorant spray.

THE NOTEBOOK VERSION

Flicking through my notebook,
I come across 'black butterflies
in the honeycomb heart of asters.'
Too poetical, I think, too rich;
or, to cite another page,
'rich as the summer rain
treacling down lush leaves;
rich as summer pudding'.

Here, I have jotted down
the title of a tome I'd seen:
Infections of Fetus and Newborn Infants.
Imagine landing, head first, in a world
where such a text is necessary...

Then further homegrown similes:
'pockmarked as a gallery wall;
permanent as the bookmark
stalled in my *Finnegans Wake;*
quick as Glenn Gould's Goldberg Variations'
- scraps in need of inspiration's heat
to weld them into shapes.
There may even be a poem
equal to the challenge
of stray sentiments such as
'There isn't much glamour
in the breadman's life'
or (a bit Larkinesque this one)
'I am what, if I had a home,
would be called homesick.'

Too much of the world
eludes the grasp of art.
There are no poems
index-linked to suffering.
Reality stings elsewhere causing real pain,

expressing itself more graphically
in sleepless nights, bad dreams,
black marks under eyes, slammed doors,
sighs, furrows, tears.

Yet the obsessiveness prevails:
persistently revising lines;
holding down an inimical job
to support a family of books;
sitting through bumptious readings;
discussing publishers; reacting to reviews;
queuing for bank drafts
to pay for foreign magazines;
making fastidious lists of superlative poets
(never reaching ten worldwide
since the winter Larkin, Graves, W.S. Graham died),
though in the end
- the phrase rejecting editors employ -
it may all go the way of shopping lists;
or, as the notebook tells it
just a smidgen histrionically:
'A day is coming soon
which even the letters you compose with
will not survive.
You must write better.
Your poems have no future.
They are only as good as they are now.
This is the time they stand the test of.'

A LONG STORY SHORT

A mane of grass was matting the centre of the lane,
ivy vaulting famine-built stone walls.
The topiary had begun outgrowing its own shapes,
its geese and lions running wild.
Flowers bloomed in fair-isle patterns;
like Bali temples, pine trees loomed.

My steps echoed against the boundaries,
then led me to a mulchy potting shed, a barn,
to the dead calf heaved on its fetid side,
left as food for the tethered guard dog
(its dangling flews now soaked
in the lukewarm trough of blood).

Larval ripples surfaced on the pool
of the calf's eye; a blue towel,
still as the sky, hung from a washing line.
A tub of mossy water fizzed with insects.
Under the weathervane, a brick belfry
without a bell threaded seams of light.

The fountain, dry as a cat's feeding bowl,
stood dreaming of endless rain.
The cool, carved hallway of the castle
flaunted no regimental flags or tapestries.
A fly's static interfered with silence
- that and the magpies hovering like bluebottles.

The day held its breath so long
it was suffocating even under trees.
I swished through sunlit, uncut meadows,
a clump of nettles serrated as crows' wings.
I had just traced a path to the boat house
when the cattle grid rattled, the guard dog snarled.

FRUIT SALAD

I. Peach

There's not much point in trying
to cultivate a sultry peach of words.
Just pass me one to stroke, to eat,
or paint it from a glowing palette,
its colours darting between apricot and apple,
flames leaping up its velvet hide.
Hold its firm, mild-scented roundness,
fondle its lightly-clothed contours,
savour its golden flesh, its flowing juice
before it starts to shrink and shrivel,
starts to wrinkle like a passion fruit.

II. Strawberry

Strawberries with whipped cream,
sun running into the lusciousness of cloud.
Slice one open like a precious stone
to reveal the pink and sugary crystal at its core.
The fruit exudes a natural, healthy red
- not the puffed-up plastic of tomatoes -
a country face with summer freckles;
its stem a garnish: parsley on beef,
verdant ferns in a bouquet of roses.
A July day provides the ideal accompaniment,
lazy as the cream dripping from the whisk.

III. Pear

Most easily hurt of fruits,
bruising under a matt coating of skin,
its inside is smooth as bath soap
or, halved, shows a perfectly-stringed lute.
It hangs in a shaft of autumn light
timeless as a bronze cathedral bell

or it disturbs the peace and drops
- a hand grenade, pin still intact -
toppling under its weight of glycerine.
We take refuge from our troubles in its sweetness,
wasps burrowing head-first through its pulp.

ALTER EGO

At times, I wish I had been able
to stay on in the home place
rounding up a few cows with the dog
having decided to give America a skip.

On Sundays, I'd take up a stick
and follow the reedy river in my suit
or lean over after Mass
to hear the chat of neighbours,
inclining toward each other
like old blotchy gravestones.

There would be a corner of hay to save,
a stack of firewood to cut and dry,
a parish club to cheer when evenings stretched,
ballads to tap a foot to in the pub.

It would be nice to see a friendly face
an odd time at the window;
a few letters - but no handwriting I'd dread.
I might have been one of those
dark characters in caps, saluting everyone,
who cycle stealthily into the town,
fixing you with a robin's scrutinising eye.

I'd keep the cottage door open from June onwards
to let in summer smells, sounds of peaty streams;
hedges blossoming with small bells;
thin-sliced wing-wrapped butterflies
alighting on my buddleia bush.

With no one's welfare but my own to care for,
I'd accept age and death with resignation.
I could have been happy that way, maybe,
walking the spotless fields on frosty mornings
or snug in knitted socks beside the grate.

On winter nights, my outside light
would perforate the dark.